US:
LOVE, LIFE, YOU, ME & EVERYTHING IN-BETWEEN

A COLLECTION OF POEMS AND SHORT STORIES

(Vers Libre)

SARITA AGARWAL

BookLeaf Publishing
India | USA | UK

US: Love, Life, You, Me & Everything In-Between

Presentation by *BookLeaf Publishing*

Web: www.bookleafpub.com
E-mail: info@bookleafpub.com

ISBN: 9789369540655

First edition 2025

DEDICATION

To my lifelines and guiding light in life's darkest moments-my ever-supportive husband, "Cherry" and my two angels, Noor and Amay.

CONTENTS

ACKNOWLEDGEMENT

Dear Ellaeenah JadeFire,
Thank you for helping me find my Inner Child.
To my friends and family,
Thank you for reading my posts and encouraging me to continue writing.

SHORT STORIES

A SNOW DAY

Zain was physically present in class,but his mind was somewhere else. He was dreaming of running through vast white fields of snow, plucking juicy red apples from snow-covered trees. In the distance he heard his teacher calling out to him, "Zain! Zaaaaiiinn!!!! You are daydreaming! Again!!??!! Get your head back into your history book,right now!!!"

Zain looked around sheepishly, apologised to his teacher and tried to focus on the topic being discussed. Suddenly the PA system in the classroom crackled and the principal's sharp voice boomed through the speakers, "Pack up your bags and rush home, it has snowed heavily in the hills and it could lead to heavy snowfall in our town as well. A Snow Day has been declared. Offices and schools are shut until further notice."

Zain couldn't believe his luck—he had just been dreaming of snow. He was the first one to run out of the class. He got on his bike and rushed home. As he parked in the driveway, he could smell the fragrance of freshly baked apple pie wafting through the air. It was almost as if his mom had read his mind. He quickly freshened up and hurried to the kitchen, where a big piece of pie awaited him. Just as he was about to take a bite, his father walked in. Soon, the three of them were laughing, talking, eating and discussing how they would spend the rest of the day.

Zain noticed that the fire in the fireplace glowed brighter that day, the apple pie tasted sweeter and the air was full of hope and happiness. It had been a while since they had sat together as a family and really connected with each other.

Tears of joy filled Zain's eyes and his heart overflowed with love. As he stepped out into the garden, snow began to fall ....

Sarita Agarwal
09.07.2021

CARRY YOUR WEIGHT

As the youngest of three brothers, I was always running to catch up with my older siblings. I would carry the cricketing gear when we got together to play cricket. I was taught the rules of the game and how to field and bat. I would carry the fishing rods and worm cans when we went on our fishing expeditions. I was taught how to put the worm on the hook and how to catch fish. I did the laundry, they did the cleaning. I did the chopping while they did the cooking and the dishes.

Yes, you could call me an assistant or an errand boy but I learnt life skills, so it wasn't all bad. As products of absentee parents,we had created our very own support system. My brothers and I were a tight-knit unit, always looking out for each other, both inside and outside our home.

My "friends" couldn't understand this "system".They often used the term "orphans" to describe us and would call my brothers "mean bullies" who were just using me. I never believed this to be true but there were times when their words got under my skin and I would feel sad and angry deep within.

Then I started noticing how my "friends" were being treated by their siblings. It seemed like the older ones were too embarrassed to hang out with the younger ones. There was no love between them.

I went home and spoke to my brothers about my observations. After hearing me out, they simply asked me to invite my "friends" to join us. "There is always room for more," they said. My heart swelled with so much more love, joy and respect for our "tight-knit unit" that any anger or sadness I may have felt, vanished into thin air.

My "friends" looked at me with incredulous disbelief when I extended the invitation to them. Over the next few weeks, they realised that their doubts were completely unfounded. They came up to me and told me they were envious of the bond that my brothers and I shared, they longed to connect with their siblings in the same way.

Now, they happily carried the gear,fishing rods and worm cans whenever needed on our joint expeditions.

Yes,all my friends had to earn their keep, just like I did.

"Lift your own weight and carry it with absolute love and joy in your heart."

Sarita Agarwal
08.07.2021

SAFE/UNSAFE

I ran. I ran really fast, I couldn't bear to look back,terrified they might be close—close enough to pull me into the car. I ran because my life depended on it. I ran because I wanted to live.

I reached the train station, bought a ticket to my hometown and quickly climbed onto an upper berth, cowering in a corner, unable to breathe. After what felt like hours, the train finally began to move. As it picked up speed, I felt like I was slowly able to breathe again. I wondered how my family would respond to my unexpected and long-overdue arrival. Would they be happy to see me? Would they be angry? Would they believe my ordeal? Would they send me back? As these questions ran through my head, I was paralysed by fear once again.

No, I won't go back. I will never go back, ever, I told myself firmly, and slowly the fear began to recede. As the train's rhythmic movement rocked me gently to sleep, the memories came flooding back.

I remember being so happy on my 10th birthday. My parents had just told me that our acquaintances in the city had agreed to support me and help me complete my studies. I would stay with them and learn about "the ways of the world". I was the envy of all my friends, the first boy from our village to go to the city, complete his education and become a "Refined Man". I would be the first one who "got out".

My nightmare started the second I stepped inside their mansion, which eventually became my prison. They locked me up and wouldn't let me contact anyone. I was fed only when I completed my chores, which began at the break of dawn and finished long after the sun had set. Any questions led to severe beatings alongside constant mental and emotional abuse. I lost track of time. Days turned into weeks, weeks into months,months into years, till my childhood became a distant memory. To survive, I did as I was told.

One night, my door opened. Someone put money in my hands and asked me to run like I had never run before, without looking back. And so, I ran.

The train lurched to a stop at my village station. I got off and ran once more, all the way home. I knocked on the door. Fear, hope, anxiety, excitement and dread were alternating within me.

My father opened the door. Upon seeing me,"You are alive?" escaped his lips before he fell to the floor, crying. My mother and the rest of the family rushed out and suddenly we were all hugging each other, wiping away our collective tears. I answered all their questions one by one. Over time, all my fears melted away.

I am Safe now, but there are countless children out there who still remain Unsafe......

Sarita Agarwal
07.07.2021

GREAT EMBRACE

I sit here, contemplating how things escalated from bad to worse in the blink of an eye. That's what it feels like to me. Faye and I had a whirlwind courtship and got married against our parent's wishes. The first year was blissful, like a scene from a beautiful rom-com. Then reality set in, life took over. There were bills to pay, groceries to buy, a house to run. Money was extremely tight. We both took on extra work, extra shifts, even on weekends, to make ends meet. We refused to reach out for help as we didn't want to hear the cliché "we told you so" from our so-called relatives and family. The pressure took a toll on "US". We were arguing, fighting, bickering, hurling abuses at each other constantly. On quite a few occasions the verbal abuse turned physical as well. We tried and failed many times to resolve our issues. Then we decided to bring a child into our world, thinking it would make "US" better.

It didn't! Things only became worse, because nothing could have prepared us for the sleepless nights, the crying, the lack of space, lack of privacy, the added bills......after the birth of our child.

A small gurgle breaks my thoughts and I turn to see Asher smiling in his sleep. He looked so angelic and beautiful, I felt a warmth engulfing my heart. I see a vision of the three of us holding hands, sitting on a picnic mat under an ancient redwood tree, sunlight streaming through its branches and leaves. I look again and now I see the light shining through Asher and he is embracing "US" tightly.

I feel a tap on my shoulder. Faye is standing next to me and I know she has had the same vision. We hold each other and feel all the pain, anger, shame, guilt and bitterness stored within "US" over the years disappear.

We turn to look at Asher, he is reaching out for us with arms wide open. We lift him up and hold each other close in a great embrace.

Sarita Agarwal
06.07.2021

THOSE WHO REMAIN

Radha and I had been together for so long that I can't even remember the exact details of our first meeting. But I can never forget how I felt...the butterflies in my stomach, the tingling in my toes, the sweaty palms and that ever so sweet pain in my heart. After the meeting, I walked home feeling like I was walking on sunshine.

I describe my life as *before Radha* and *after Radha*. Before Radha, my life was a complete mess, with no beginning, no middle and no end; everything was all jumbled up. After Radha, I found direction, I found a purpose and above all,I found unconditional love.

I sit here now, looking out the window, watching my two absolutely beautiful children run around and play in the first rains of the monsoon. I feel her presence all around them, watching over and caring for them. As I feel her strength and absence within me, that sweet pain returns to my heart, so very-very deeply.

The virus affected us both, I came back but Radha moved on to whatever comes next.

I am Rohan and I am one of those who remain.........

Sarita Agarwal
05.07.2021

WORTHY SUCCESSOR

The majestic male Elephant, Oba, walked with quiet dignity, deep in thought. His tusks were white and so long that they almost touched the ground. All the elephants in the herd watched with awe as he passed by. He was a grand old elephant who had watched over his herd with love, kindness, wisdom and compassion since his mother passed on this responsibility to him, not another female, just before she left for her heavenly abode. Oba had accepted his mother's last wish, curbing his natural instinct of moving away from the herd and leading a solitary life. Now, it was time for him to pass on this mantle to a worthy successor. But he was facing a dilemma. He had spoken to all the elephants in the herd except for Nandi, whom he felt was far too young and not yet capable of replacing him.

He wondered how his mother had been so sure that he would be a wise and responsible leader.

Oba walked further away from the herd and deeper into the forest, lost in his thoughts. Suddenly, he felt a sharp, searing pain in his back, which quickly spread to his entire body. A rope was thrown over his head and tied around his feet and he fell to the ground with a resounding thud. He could hear the poachers all around him and see the glint of their blades in the moonlight. However, he was too weak and too old to fight them off and he watched helplessly as they began to saw off his tusks. Oba drifted away, if this was to be his last moment then so be it, he thought.

Suddenly, the poachers screamed.One by one, Oba saw them flying in the air, landing far from him and running away without looking back.The rope around his neck was removed and his feet were free. But he could not get up as the pain remained as sharp as ever. He had been shot with poisoned arrows.

Oba lifted his head to see who his saviour was. A beautiful majestic elephant was standing next to him and she glowed as if all of Luna's light was shining through her. It was Nandi. And in that moment, he knew she was the one.

Oba trumpeted loudly to announce his decision. The whole herd gathered around him and prayed for his last journey, into the light.

Oba left his body with peace in his heart and joined his ancestors amongst the stars.

Sarita Agarwal
04.07.2021

COMMUNICATION

Mia and Ravi were best friends, absolutely inseparable, attached at the hip. They lived in each other's houses, went to school together, came home together, did their homework together and got up to mischief together. When people found out that they weren't related, they were completely shocked. Over time they had even started resembling each other physically. Their parents considered them to be two souls in one body. They were like twins born to different parents.

Then Mia met Jai and suddenly their relationship changed. Mia and Jai were always together, and Ravi started feeling like an outsider, a stranger. He could not understand this change. He started wallowing in his own misery, he lost interest in everything around him. He started falling ill constantly and eventually stopped getting out of bed altogether.

Mia came over one day to speak to him after Ravi's mother reached out to her. Mia saw Ravi and started crying. Seeing this, Ravi also began to cry. When the tears eventually stopped, they both hugged each other really tightly. Mia asked why Ravi hadn't shared his feelings about her relationship with Jai instead of keeping everything bottled up and making himself so very ill. She apologised for not asking about this change in him, for not reaching out earlier. She asked Ravi to tell her everything honestly and openly without holding anything back. And he did. He told her how hurt, abandoned, hopeless and lost he felt, like suddenly he was only surrounded by darkness, like he was drowning in the middle of the ocean without a life jacket or a boat to hold on to. He had lost the will to live because he felt Mia was not in his life anymore.

Mia listened to every word with tears in her eyes. She told him that Jai was the love of her life and she knew it the second she'd looked into his eyes. But she loved Ravi too and he would always remain her best friend for life. She had been so upset with Ravi for ignoring her, not talking to her, not accepting Jai whenever she tried to bring him into their friendship, so she had stopped reaching out. Just like him,she also felt like a part of her heart had been torn out when she lost her connection with Ravi.

Mia and Ravi spoke for hours and hours and they both understood the importance of communication—the importance of sharing their feelings without doubt and hesitation—and promised to never take each other for granted and never stop talking to each other ever.

Ravi came out of his room. Jai was downstairs,waiting patiently. They looked at each other and exchanged a long, heartfelt hug and spoke for what felt like eternity.

Mia, Jai and Ravi remained as thick as thieves for the rest of their lives despite the ups and downs that came their way.

Sarita Agarwal
03.07.2021

THE RED BALL

Once upon a time, there was a little boy who was very lonely. Whenever he would go to the park near his house and try to talk to other kids, they would laugh at him, make fun of him, and call him names like "basti boy" and "ragster". He would come home in tears and ask his mom why the children were so mean to him. She would just ask him to ignore them as they did not deserve his friendship. She always told him that when someone is truly worthy of being your friend, they will accept you as you are without caring about anything else.

One day, the lonely boy found a little red ball outside his house. He picked it up and looked around but could not see anyone to whom it might belong. He decided to keep it, playing with it by bouncing it against a wall every day. And he was never ever lonely again....

Sarita Agarwal
02.07.2021

THE FIRE

Life was simple, life was beautiful and we were happy. Our home overlooked the meadows, interspersed with tall green trees, yellow grass and flowers the colour of the rainbow. A lilting blue stream flowed past us. We sat together as a family, watching many sunsets and sunrises.

And then one evening, we saw smoke rising in the distance, it seemed darker and more threatening than usual.The sky had turned an ominous shade of red. Before we could react, the other animals rushed past us urging us to hurry as the fire was consuming everything in its path. Soon the collective shrieking of all beings filled the night sky. I gathered my pride and we ran as fast as we could, hoping and praying that Uru and the other lions had reached a place of safety. We managed to outrun the fire without any casualties but the other families lost many loved ones.

Time passed by very slowly and then one day,rain pelted down from the sky and unleashed a roaring flood that finally put an end to the blazing inferno. We watched with reverence, love and prayers, as Gaia cleansed herself. When we began the long walk home, we could feel the heaviness, anger and pain that still remained within our beloved Mother Earth.

I saw Uru in the distance, looking over what was left of our home.The meadows, the trees, the grass and the flowers were now the darkest shade of black. The once-lilting stream flowed past us sluggishly, joylessly, full of gloom and despair. Uru saw me and we ran into each other's arms. All the fear, pain and sorrow that we had experienced melted away and we could clearly see the path that lay before us.

A meeting was called for all the beings of the forest."Life goes on but we must recognise the error of our ways and change. We must protect what is left and rebuild that which has been destroyed," we said to all gathered. Everyone got together and started the process of rebuilding with hope,love and unshakable faith in their hearts.

The fire affected us all. We have changed, we have adapted and we live in peace and harmony with each other and our beloved Mother. We now understand that "One cannot Exist without the Other,we are One,we are the Other."

The humans tried really hard but they could not control the fire or the flood that followed. They struggled with all their might but the wrath of nature, once unleashed, cannot be overcome by Machines and Inventions alone...I am yet to see a change in their behaviour, in fact,they seem to be on the verge of forgetting....

I hope and pray every single day that humans truly realise the error of their ways and change before it's too late for all of US.......

"We cannot live in denial any longer, we cannot exist in isolation, we are an integral part of the eco-system and we must change now."

Sarita Agarwal
22.07.2021

POEMS

AFTER THE FALL

I step away and the cracks begin to reappear,
I have a yearning desire to rush back,
I am gripped by a familiar fear,
Will I be able to bridge the gap?
Will I be able to catch it all before the fall?
Will I be able to pick up the scattered pieces of the wall?
Should I pay heed to this inner call?
Or
Should I hold back the compulsion to be near?
Can this be the need of the hour?
Are the cracks the source of all our power?
After the Fall,
That's when the light seeps in,
After the Fall,
That's when the inner voice awakens,
Step away, leave the door ajar,
Watch over from afar
And let the light in.

Sarita Agarwal
04.06.2022

A PHOTOGRAPH OF US

I go back in time,
Right back to when we held each
other so passionately,
The world fades away,
The surroundings blur,
I step into a space that's just ours,
I can still feel myself tremble,
I can still feel the knots in my stomach,
I can still feel my heart begin to beat with a different
rhythm,
I can still see every inch of your face,
Your eyes are the windows to my soul,
Your smile fills with light, the darkest corners of my
mind,
Your voice is a balm to all my aches,
I wait lovingly,
I wait patiently,
I wait endlessly......,
To hold you in a tight embrace,
To shower you with all my kisses,
I feel a flood of tears wet my cheeks,
I snap back to reality,

I look at the photograph in my hands,
I hold it in a tight embrace,
I shower it with all my kisses,
I gently wipe away my tears,
A tender smile forms at the corner of my lips as I step out into the world.

Sarita Agarwal
30.05.2022

PRAYING FOR TIME

Watching the clock,
Constantly seeing,
Constantly hearing,
The ticking of time,
Watching the pendulum
Swing from side to side,
Watching the hands
Move from second to second,minute to minute,hour to hour,
Watching the days,weeks,months,years
Turn into decades,decades into centuries,
Watching time go by,
Watching acts of progression,
Watching acts of regression,
Waiting for everlasting changes,
Waiting…,
Waiting…,
Constantly waiting,
Praying for time,
Praying for some more time……

Sarita Agarwal
15.05.2022

BLANK PAGE

Feel free to write on me,
Write on me all your love,
Write on me all your hate,
Write on me all your tears,
Write on me all your fears,
Write on me all your desires,
Write on me all your rage,
Write on me when you can't speak the words,
Write on me the unheard,
Write on me when the lines are blurred,
Write on me and create a wondrous space where all of you is safe,
Feel free to write on me,
I am your Blank Page.

Sarita Agarwal
13.05.2022

THE FABRIC OF HUMANITY

Across generations,
When we witness, when
we experience
Hate, anger, violence and
abuse,
Deeply rooted physical,
mental and emotional pain
ensues,
Fissures, Fractures, Cracks in
all dimensions,
Appear beyond the horizon
Where the first rays of the rising sun illuminate the
dawn sky,
And below the horizon
Where the last rays of the setting sun herald the
approaching night,
In and out, out and In,
Turmoil, Trauma, Terror spin,
Doubt, panic and fear reign supreme,
Slowly weaving their threads into the fabric of humanity,

Take a step back and find clarity,
With gratitude and honour, accept and acknowledge what is,
Truly believe and manifest change,
With grace, kindness and relentless determination, sans conditions,
Fill each fissure, fracture, crack with hope, love and faith,
Ever so patiently,
Reweave the very fabric of humanity,

Sarita Agarwal
02.05.2022

IN MEMORIAM

You left us exactly a year ago,
Time has passed us by, fast yet slow,
We have borne witness to so much change,
Hope, love, faith, gain,
Despair, loss, death, pain,
We took it all in our stride,
Because we knew that you are by our side,
We feel your warm embrace
Whenever tears flood our face,
When our burdened heart feels heavy
The weight you help us carry,
Your guidance is in every silent whisper,
Your love is in every silent prayer,
Within us you will forever reside,
Watching over us with your ever-smiling loving eyes.

"Love you, Mom"

Sarita Agarwal
30.04.2022

WITHIN THE VORTEX

Dark darker darkest darkness,
Sinking slowly,
Into a bottomless pit,
Swirling, spinning uncontrollably,
Within the vortex,
Anger erupts like lava from a long-simmering Volcano,
Deep-rooted anguish expelled,
Peace descends like snowflakes falling gently from the winter clouds,
Bright brighter brightest light,
Rising slowly,
Up towards the sky,
Feel,
Forgive,
Love,
Embrace,
Stay grounded,not rooted to the spot,
Stay connected,to the core of who you are,
In the midst of chaos,
In the midst of harmony,

In the midst of anarchy,
In the midst of order,
Let go and observe,
Surrender within the Vortex.

Sarita Agarwal
13.04.2022

UNLOAD

Continuously
The pressure is too high,
Constantly
The weight is too heavy,
I am unable to move physically,
But my mind is a completely different story,
It works itself into a frenzy,
My heart begins to drown,
Within me, screams resound,
I feel like I will explode,
I need to learn how to unload,
I rise up, looking for a way out,
I find a peak impossible to surmount,
I turn around and dive deep deep within,
The unlit maze sends me into a spin,
I take a deeper breath and push through the dark,
I finally reach my silent heart,
With all my strength, I try to reignite its spark,
Beat by Beat
I can feel the rhythm coming back,
Beat by Beat
A warmth embraces me from head to toe,

Beat by Beat
A love engulfs me down to my very core,
A light from within emits with such force,
I disintegrate and connect with the highest source,
I am reborn,
I am renewed,
I am restored,
Step by Step
I am learning to unload.

Sarita Agarwal
02.03.2022

THE VOICES IN THE DARK

The voices in the dark
They speak,
The voices in the dark
Go deep,
The voices in the dark
Awaken when you sleep,
The voices in the dark
Tell tales,
Of times gone by,
Of things left behind,
Of our fears,
And our tears,
The voices in the dark
Echo our unknowns,
The voices in the dark
Speak what remains unspoken,
If you choose to listen
With your heart,
If you choose to listen
With your soul,
The voices in the dark will mend what's broken,
Listen well, be awakened.

Sarita Agarwal
25.03.2022

ACROSS THE ROOM

Across the room,
I saw you look at me,
You sent my heart and my head into a spin,
Your smile set fire to my skin,
I held my breath,
Without a word,
Without a touch,
We saw all that we could be,
Across the room.

Sarita Agarwal
25.03.2022

THE CHAOS

The heart aches,
It aches like it's never
going to stop hurting,
It aches like it might just stop
beating,
You try to move forward,
But yet again, unexpected news pulls you back into the
past,
Within and without, there is only chaos,
You wonder, how long will it last this time?
You wonder, will it ever be fine?
You begin to question your existence,
You ponder, can there ever be Existence sans chaos?
Observe the patterns,
Observe the interconnectedness,
The unexpected news is not so "unexpected," is it?
Remember, Existence is chaos,
Without chaos nothing can evolve,
Learn to Breathe within the chaos,
Learn to Breathe within the trauma,
Learn to Breathe within the pain,
Learn to Breathe within the love,

Learn to Breathe within the joy,
Learn to Breathe within the laughter,
Don't get attached to outcomes,
Don't get overwhelmed by emotions,
Don't get stuck within the events,
Feel each one,
Experience each one,
Process each one,
Don't let the outcomes or emotions consume you,
Don't suppress or bypass them,
Move through each one,
Accept, acknowledge, honour each one,
Spread, share the love and light within,
Send the darkness out into the cosmos to turn into light,
Truly believe events are happening *for* you and not *to* you,
They occur for your highest good,for the highest good of all,
Time and again, we are reminded—
NOW is all we have,
NOW is yesterday's future,
NOW is tomorrow's past,
Our past and future coexist in this very moment,
Don't wait for everything to fall into place,
Everything is already as it should be,
Embrace the chaos,
Clear the slate,
Clean the slate,
Start NOW and don't stop.

Sarita Agarwal
15.03.2022

THE ABYSS

Is it?
A blessing or a curse,
This unending thirst,
This cut-throat urge,
This need to rush,
To constantly push
Myself to the edge,
I stand on the brink
Without a blink,
Staring into the dark abyss,
Is that a light I see
Calling out to me,
To fearlessly
Take a step
And set myself free,
Is it?
A blessing or a curse.....

Sarita Agarwal
21.03.2022

SHAKE OFF THESE CHAINS

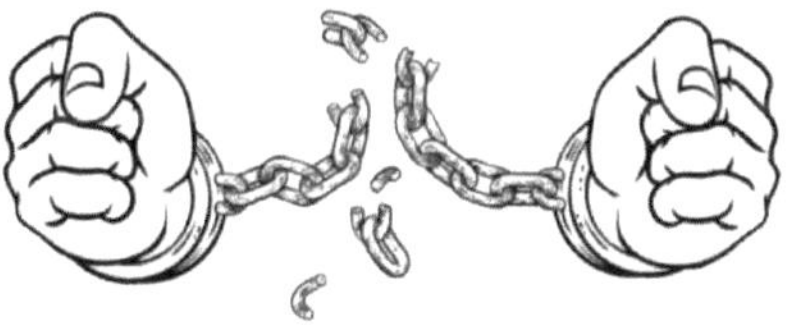

It's been a year, and
what a year it's been,
The things we heard,
The things we saw,
The things that cannot
be Unseen,
The unimaginable,
The unexpected,
The unthinkable,
We climbed insurmountable mountains,
We crossed broken bridges,
We overcame every obstacle in our paths,
We continued forward despite repeated setbacks,
We conquered it all,
We stayed the course,
With love, hope, unity and faith,
Irrespective of what's on our plates,
We will weather the inevitable storms,
We will soak up the sun,
We will dance in the rain,
We will arise and shake off these chains,
Together.

Sarita Agarwal
14.03.2022

DIE IN SOMEONE ELSE'S SKIN...

Who am I?
What is my identity?
Someone that I
aspire to be?
Something that is expected of
me?
Someone that I am not?
Something that everyone wants?
When did I lose my way?
When did I stop having a say?
When did I begin to chase the same butterfly?
When did I stop looking up at the sky?
When did I start walking with the crowd?
A chill runs down my spine, I shiver,
I don't recognise the reflection in the mirror,
I see a shell,
I see a ghost,
I see a dark shadow underneath the lamppost,
I see a caricature in someone else's never-ending dream,
I can't wake myself up even if I scream,
My very existence is at stake,
I need to pinch myself awake,

I need to undo this mistake,
I need to find myself again,
I need to go deep within,
I need to go right down to my very core,
I can't keep up with this version of myself any more,
Now is when I begin,
I can't, I won't
Die in someone else's skin......

Sarita Agarwal
13.03.2022

MY HEART AND I

Shattered, cracked,
The countless pieces of my heart
Lie scattered across the floor,
There is nothing left within,
There is nothing left to fight for,
I can't find the strength,
I can't find the will,
To gather all the pieces,
To stitch them back together,
I let them lie,
I leave them be,
I watch as they get trampled on,
I watch as they get kicked about like debris,
I watch it all unfold repeatedly,silently,
I close my eyes and begin to float away,
Disconnecting from my surroundings,
Detaching from my reality,
I feel a hug, I feel a tug,
Pulling me back to the ground,
I see my taped-up heart calling me back,
I can still see all the cracks,
I can still see all the abrasions,

I can't go back,
I turn around,ready to bound,
As my feet lift off the ground
I see a blinding white light burst forth from each crack,
It fills me with warmth,
It fills me with love,
It fills me with hope,
It fills me with renewed strength,
With my feet firmly on the ground,
I lovingly embrace my heart,
I make a promise to never ever let go,
I promise to carry my own tune,
I promise to sing my own song,
Till infinity and beyond.

Sarita Agarwal
09.03.2022

MASTERPIECE

Turn back time,
Rewind the moments lived,
Go right back to when it all started,
Go right back to the moment of birth,
Get some popcorn,
Sit back, relax, put your feet up,
And press play to start the movie,
Watch your story, your life's work,
Your very own masterpiece,
Unfold before your very eyes,
The script,
The dialogues,
The editing,
The direction,
All the emotions,
All the drama,
All the plots,
All the unexpected twists,
All the characters,
All the paths,
All your choices,
See it all with eyes anew,

Recognise your role,
Continue to play it with aplomb,
The movie isn't over yet,
Remember, there is no end,
Your choices define your now and what lies ahead,
Choose wisely, my friend.

Sarita Agarwal
06.03.2022

MARCH ON

March On
To the drum roll,
March On
To the beat,

March On
With your heart,
March On
With your feet,

March On
Into the setting sun,
March On
Into the night,

March On
As the sun rises,
March on
Into the light,

March On
Through the blinding rain,
March On
Into the Hurricane,

March On
When in pain,
March On
Till only love remains,

March On
Till you come to a standstill,
And find me there, you will —
With arms wide open,
Waiting patiently for you to stand beside me,
In all your glory.

Sarita Agarwal
05.03.2022

DAILY STRUGGLE...

On the tip…,
On the verge…,
On the edge…,
Should I?
Shouldn't I?
Will I?
Won't I?
Will they stare?
Why do I care?
I fumble,
I slip,
I tumble,
Can they even see?
Do they even care?
I was ensnared in this daily struggle,
My entire existence consumed by this juggle,
Life passed me by in a frantic blur,
I sat waiting for a silver lining to appear,
I look back now and smile from ear to ear,
If it weren't for this struggle,

If it weren't for this juggle,
I wouldn't be where I am today,
I wouldn't be *here*.

Sarita Agarwal
01.03.2022

IS IT TRULY WORTH IT?

Pakistani...
Bangladeshi...
Indian...
Srilankan...
Tibetan...
Bhutanese...
Indonesian...
Malaysian...
Thai...
Singaporean...
Chinese...
Japanese...
Korean...
Asian...
Russian...
Ukrainian...
European...
African...
American...
Native American...
Hawaiian...
Australian...

Black...
White...
Brown...
Old...
Young...
Teenager...
Toddler...
Infant...
In utero...
Men...
Women...
Children...
Soldier...
Veteran...
Animal...
Bird...
Bee..
Insect...
Plant...
Tree...
Forest...
Earth...
Water...
Air...
Mother Earth...
Living...
Non-living...
Human...
Non-human..
Being...

All life Matters...
The price of Peace...
The cost of WAR...
The price we PAY...
Is it truly worth it?

Sarita Agarwal
04.03.2022

US

Predictably unpredictable...
Unforgivingly forgivable...
Complicatedly simple...
Shallowly deep...
Turbulently peaceful...
Unlovingly loveable...
The calm within the storm...
The order in the chaos...
Lift the veil and you will see ME.

Sarita Agarwal
28.02.2022

THE LIGHT ON THE MEADOW

The light on the meadow filters through the clouds,
Illuminating all that lies upon the ground,
Giving much-needed respite from the unrelenting
coldness that surrounds,
What should be, appears so very clear,
What should be, appears so very near,
Then the path begins to crack,
Three steps forward, two steps back,
Everything begins to quake,
We begin to doubt,
We begin to fear,
We begin to hesitate,
This is a pattern we must choose to break,
Resist the urge to get sucked back into the shadow,
Keep moving forward towards the light on the meadow,
Recognise the chaos for what it is,
Recognise the ripples for what they are,
For they are a part of the cosmic light,
Misunderstood and unseen by the human sight,
When time and space bend into each other,
And the mind begins to work for the heart,
Love will unify all,

The light on the meadow will begin to emanate through each crack,
The light on the meadow will reflect off each ripple,
The light on the meadow will begin to radiate from all,
Illuminating all that IS,
All is crystal clear
We are moving forward,
Without any doubt, without any fear

Sarita Agarwal
23.02.2022

AS I LAY MY HEAD TO REST

The pillars...
The poles...
The trees...
The road...
The honks...
The wind...
The sunlight...
All whizz past me,
As I lay my head to rest,
A calm begins to descend,
All movements come to a standstill,
I hear the silence within the sounds,
I shut my eyes…,
And drift into a selfless state of sleep.

Sarita Agarwal
21.02.2022

BRIGHTEST OF BLUES

You and I,…
Sitting under the starlight…,
Gazing at the moon shining so bright…,
We get lost looking into each other's eyes…,
Talking past midnight…,
Watching the sunrise…,
The time just flies by…,
I go back whenever I close my eyes…,
I never wanted this moment to end…,
I painted a picture inside my head…,
How did we ever drift apart?
I can't even remember the start…,
I sit under the starlight…,
Gazing at the moon shining so bright…,
I get lost looking back in time…,
Thinking past midnight…,
Watching the sunrise…,
The time just flies by…,
I look up with my eyes open wide…,
The moment has passed…,
The picture has faded…,
I see the brightest of blues and smile...

Sarita Agarwal
17.02.2022

WHAT WOULD MAKE YOU HAPPY?

I read this question and my mind
raced to answer,
It shouted: peace, love, oneness,
unity for ALL,
But my heart felt heavy,there was
no response,
These were just words,
Saying them out loud did
not make me happy,
Thinking them did not make me happy,
In fact I felt weighed down and unhappy,
Achieving these objectives seemed like an
insurmountable task,
Dejection began to rain down on me,
I felt lost, so very lost,
As I sat,
Wondering where,when,how do I even begin,
As I sat,
Questioning all that I had been learning,
A realisation struck me like lightning,
I became sharply aware of each and every emotion I was
experiencing,

The weight lifted and the clouds parted,
The light shone through brighter than ever before,
Each ray questioned me,
"Are you truly at peace within?
Do you truly love all of Your Self?
Have you truly let go of separation, divisions, labels, judgement, rage within Your Self?
Have you truly let go of the need to seek approval outside of Your Self?"
Doubt and fear began to engulf me,
But I responded with relentless, brutal self-reflection,
Each ray spoke, encouraging me to look deeper within,
"Remember, where there is doubt,fear and hesitation, there also lies recognition, realisation and awareness of Your Self,
You have come a long way, but there is a longer way to go still,
Continue, dear child,
Don't lose heart, stay on the path,
Get back on even if you falter,
Get back on even if you fall,
And it will lead to peace, love, unity, oneness within YOU,
And that which makes YOU happy will be for ALL".

Sarita Agarwal
05.02.2022

TIME

Seconds merge into minutes,
Minutes into hours,
Hours into days,
Days merge into weeks,
Weeks into months,
Months into years,
Years into decades.....,
Time flies by
All that remains,
Are moments we shared,
The memories we created,
I look back now and smile,
I look ahead and smile even more,
I look at the present and my heart overflows with love and gratitude,
We have come a long way, but there is a longer way to go still,
May we rise after every fall,
May we continue to embrace it all,
May we continue to shine our light with love in our hearts,
Together, the journey continues....,
Always and Forever.

Sarita Agarwal
10.02.22

AND THEN THERE WAS

No one
Left to shed a tear,
Left to fear,
Left to fight,
Left to love,
Left to hate,
Left to hug,
Left to push away,
Left to resent,
Left to blame,
Left to judge,
Left to shame,
Left to maim,
And then there was,
Not a thing left to label,
Not a thing left to surmount,
Only Love remained,
It all merged,
It all became one,
An endless ocean of consciousness,

Each one a drop,
No different from the other,
No separation,
Only unification.

Sarita Agarwal
26.01.2022

AN UNSPOKEN CONNECTION

I sit amidst the trees,
Breathing, Listening, Feeling,
Two Bulbuls come and sit on a branch near me,
We watch, we observe each other quietly, closely,
Between the three of us,
We share, we feel, we know,
Without any exchange,
Within us lies,
An unspoken bond,
An unspoken understanding,
An unspoken connection,
That can only be felt in our hearts,
That can only be felt in stillness,
Calm the mind,
Calm the heart,
Calm the spirit,
Release the fear,
And it will appear.

Sarita Agarwal
15.01.2022

SEIZE THE DAY

You feel like you are
up against a wall,
You try and you try
to climb,
But you only slip and fall,
You plan to bring old patterns to an end,
They seem to disappear but then become
the new trend,
You begin to wonder if this will ever end,
Suddenly a thought appears that's heaven sent,
Don't focus on the what's, how's and why's,
Joyous moments will pass you by,
Never let the love fade away,
Unconditional and Unshakeable is the only way,
That's when you seize the day.

Sarita Agarwal
24.12.2021

THE UNDERBELLY

The dark side,
The lowest of the low,
All that lies deep within,
All that lies deep below,
We try and try to push it away,
We try and try to cover it up each day,
And then the fears set in,
What if the unseen is seen?
These fears cloud all the light,
These fears suppress what is right,
These fears ensure we forget our might,
These fears make us give up the fight,
Strengthen the underbelly,
Embrace the underbelly,
Shower it with love,
Shower it with kindness,
Share with it your strength,
Share with it your faith,
Share with it your empathy,
Share with it your kindness,

Witness the miracle of existence,
Watch the Underbelly step into the light,
Watch the Underbelly rise and take flight.

Sarita Agarwal
18.11.2021

THE COLLECTIVE

This world that we see through the eyes of *me*,
Cannot be all that you want and need it to *be*,
Feel the pulse of the Earth beneath your feet in every step that you take,
Feel the life of the world fill your lungs in every breath that you receive,
Feel the love of the cosmos fill your heart
Through every kind and empathetic thought and action,for yourself and others,
Question the set norms,
Don't criticise, think critically,
Don't judge or allow yourself to be judged,
Don't compare or fill yourself with competition,
Don't label or allow yourself to be labelled,
Achieve, soar, recreate, renew, restore,
Live and lead a life full of abundance, wealth, health, love and happiness,
Together, not at the cost of the other,
End this cycle of corruption,
End this cycle of misrepresentation,
End this cycle of separation,
End this cycle of blame,

End this cycle of shame,
End this cycle of guilt,
End this cycle of pain,
End this here and now,
Going forward, take a vow,
To see this world through the eyes of the collective,
To create a tsunami that changes the mindset of one and all,
Start now or the Collective will fall...

Sarita Agarwal
18.08.2021

THE SLIPPERY SLOPE

The slippery slope,
Just slipped,
Right from underneath my feet,
It took me with it, gently to
my surprise,
Not with anger or with spite,
I felt it carry me over the rivers
and ravines,
As if I were seated on a bed of clouds all mine,
I floated away, over the trees, the hill and the plains,
The birds flew past me, the birds flew with me, till the
very end,
Or was it the beginning?I couldn't say with absolute
certainty,
Even though I was moving, time was standing still,
I reached what I presume was my destination,
And walked purposefully into the light,
I felt only deep endless love surround me, engulf me,
envelope me,
I heard the words of love echo all around me,
"Welcome home, my dearest child,
The journey continues, there are no hellos and goodbyes,
Embrace love,embrace light, you are free of these earthly ties,
Now Shakti will rise."

Sarita Agarwal
01.08.2021

A RAINY DAY

Oh! I can't wait for a rainy day,
To slip on my rain boots,
To put on my raincoat,
To open my umbrella,
And rush outside to play,
I jump in the muddy puddles,
With absolute glee,
Without a care about the mud that splashes onto me,
This is the one day my mom lets me run free,
For now, I look out of my window and wait impatiently,
For the pitter-patter of raindrops to fall all around me.

Sarita Agarwal
23.06.2021

PURPLE PAPER KITE

I sit in my garden and look up at the sky,
I see a purple paper kite floating by,
There is no one pulling at its string,
The kite is moving with the flow of the wind,
I trace its path, I follow it as far as I can see,
Soon it lands on a Banyan tree,
To my utter delight,
I feel this sudden urge to write,
The words come pouring out of me,
I feel my soul stirring,
Simply because I chanced upon a purple paper kite.

"We all have a purpose, find your purpose and let love envelop you inside out."

Sarita Agarwal
12.07.2021

I AM STILL

I flow like the River, yet I am still,
I blow like the Wind, yet I am still,
I swirl like the Hurricane, yet I am still,
I spin like the Tornado, yet I am still,
I shake like the Earth, yet I am still,
I orbit the Sun,yet I am still,
I rise up like the Tsunami, yet I am still,
I erupt like the Volcano, yet I am still,
I whirl like the Dervish, yet I am still,
I breathe, yet I am still,
I am ever-changing,
I am ever-moving,
I am continuously evolving,
Yet I am still,
Feel the stillness within,
When surrounded by conflict,
When surrounded by peace,
When surrounded by hate,
When surrounded by Love,
Feel the stillness within,
In each breath, in each moment, in each action,
Feel the stillness within.

Sarita Agarwal
12.07.2021

THE LIST

Have you ever looked in the mirror and
asked yourself,
Who is the most important person in
your life?
Take a look,
What do you see?
Is it your children?
Is it your husband?
Is it your wife?
Is it your entire family?
All cannot be further from what the answer should be,
Where are YOU in the scheme of things?
Where do YOU figure on the list?
Why are YOU not even on the list?
Reflect on these questions for a while,
Don't be in a hurry, take your time,
Now to this advice, do pay heed,
You have imprisoned yourself in constant worry,
You have imprisoned yourself in the others' needs,
You have forgotten your personal identity,
Remind yourself of who YOU are,
Accept yourself as a whole,

With all your scars and all your missed goals,
With all your hate and all your pain,
With all your love and all your gains,
With all your anger and all your fears,
With all your laughter and all your tears,
With all your shame and all your guilt,
Remember all, remember how each one felt,
You are human,
You are flawed,
Forgive yourself despite it all,
Make this exercise a daily task,
Look in the mirror and always ask,
Who is the most important person in your life?
If the answer still remains the same,
Reflect within and start all over again,
When you truly put yourself first,
When you truly embrace yourself at your worst,
The list, you will not need,
Everyone and everything within YOU and outside will be freed.

Sarita Agarwal
28.06.2021

FLY SOLO

I am learning to fly,
I just got my wings,
I will sail through the sky,
I just got my wings,
I will survive,
Because you taught me to trust my instincts,
I am learning to fly,
I will spread my wings,
I promise myself to explore and try new things,
I am learning to fly,
I just got my wings,
I promise myself to always try,
In every situation,
In every complication,
In happiness and in sorrow,
I promise myself to never ever let go,
I am learning to fly,
I am flying Solo.

Sarita Agarwal
29.06.2021

LET LOVE IN

Love love love love
Dwells all around us—
IN
The plants and the trees,
The birds and the bees,
The clouds and the breeze,
The sun and the sky,
The moon and stars,
The oceans and their waves,
The ripples in the rivers,
The swells in the lakes,
The icing on the cake,
The mess the kids make,
The moment we apply the brakes,
The blessings when we sneeze,
The hugs when we meet,

Just look a little more closely,
Just breathe a little more deeply,
Just feel a little more intensely,
Let love conquer all,
All your insecurities,

All your fears,
All your self-doubt,
Let the showers of love embrace you inside out,
Live as love,
Let love,all negativity surmount,
Let Love IN.

Sarita Agarwal
22.06.2021

THE SEARCH

How do I begin to describe how I feel?
I am restless, I feel trapped,
My mind seems to be on the verge of collapse,
The thoughts rushing through my head, float away,
Just as they appear to be within my grasp,
I follow them to see where they might be,
I look amidst the forest that surrounds me,
My gaze cannot penetrate its density,
I continue the search,
I come across a lake that calls out to me,
"Immerse yourself, and then you will see",
I am drenched from my head to my feet,
And yet I cannot find what I seek,
I continue the search,
I hear the sounds of nature reverberate all around me,
"Look and Listen with your soul", they call to me,
I try and I try and yet I cannot hear,
What to them seems so very clear,
I continue my search,
Somewhere deep down I can feel that I am closer than before,

But there is doubt,there is hesitation,I am not sure,
I look up towards the sun-kissed sky,
I see the wind, the clouds,as they pass me by,
Exhausted I sit still on a rock nearby,
Hoping that this will help me regain my strength to
soon retry,
The day turns into night, time flies by,
I lie down,close my eyes with a long weary sigh,
Suddenly from somewhere very deep within me,my
Inner child calls out to me,
"Ah! Finally! You hear me, you see me,
Now truly listen, with your entire being,
You grow, You read, You write, You learn,
You live your life, You earn,
But do you bring this growth and learning to your
living?
Or is it all only expecting, hoping and wishing?
What you learn you must truly apply,
Or that which you seek will pass you by,"
A warmth, a glow begins to fill my chest,
I see now with renewed sight,
The forest, the lake, the rock, the sounds are all within
me,
I am All, All is me,
This realisation ends my outward quest,
Reconnect with yourself,
Awaken your inner child,
Find your sight,
We are all interconnected through energy, through light,

Together we search,
Together we find,
Together, we rise above these worldly ties that cloud our minds,
How do I begin to describe how I feel?
I am at peace with myself, I am free,
The search within continues.

Sarita Agarwal
18.06.2021

FOR YOU, MOM

There were days of darkness,
There were days that felt like
endless nights,
But when you walked
beside me,
I always saw the sun rise,
I saw your struggles,
I saw your conflicts,
I saw your strength and your will to fight,
I saw your happy memories,
I saw all the love that you had to give,
I saw the ebb and flow of the life you lived,
I saw your childlike innocence,
I saw your need for discipline,
I saw your need to wander,
I saw your need to explore,
I saw the deep sorrow, when with your mind and your body,you could do no more,
I saw your mischievous smiles,
I saw you break the norms,
I saw your eyes light up when the children cooked up a storm,

I saw YOU clear as day,
I saw your need to be free,
Free of all the pain and boundaries,
I see now,
You needed us to let YOU go...
So that YOU could let go,
I see YOU now,
Flying freely up above,
Spreading joy as you move,
Sharing all your light and love,
In the Circle of Life,
This is merely a physical separation,
In our hearts you will forever remain,
Until Mom,we meet again.

Sarita Agarwal
16.05.2021

AN OUTPOURING OF GRIEF

Just yesterday, it felt like everything was finally going to be okay. Things were moving in the right direction. Things were settling down. And then, all of a sudden, the world around me collapsed, caved in. There was no warning, no softened blow. It was one gut punch after another. There was barely any time to surface for air before I got pulled under again and again.

I was overwhelmed, choking, unable to breathe. I couldn't focus on what was in front of me and everything spun out of control. And then, I let go, I stopped resisting and just surrendered to every emotion, every feeling, anything at all that was surfacing. I let it flow out of me like a gushing river, a tsunami, a tornado...I let it all out. There was no beginning or end, no structure, no form and no code. It all just poured out of me. And I felt free, like I had never felt before, I felt a light inhale the unending darkness that was consuming me from within...........

Sarita Agarwal
12.05.2021

FREE FALLIN'

I am free fallin'........
Completely untethered,
Caught up in wave after
wave.....
Falling freely in any and
every weather,
Moving from place to
place,
Moving from space to
space,
Trying to make sense of it all,
Trying to fill in the gaps,
Trying to complete the puzzle,
Trying but failing at all costs,
Where do we even begin,
To tie the loose ends,
How do we even begin to get past,
At some point we must start,
Jump right into the deep end and swim fast,
Will it all fall into place?
Will we see a picture painted on the landscape?
Will we ever begin to feel?

Will we ever begin to heal?
I can't find the answers,
I can't even begin to see,
I hope and I pray time will show the way,
The passage will explain,
How or why things are,
How or why some things remain,
For now I am free fallin'........
Completely untethered,
Caught up in wave after wave......

Sarita Agarwal
10.05.2021

COME WHAT MAY

I remember standing next to you on a balcony,
Overlooking the fields of dreams,
The times were full of love,
The smiles were full of hope,
There was no judgement, no expectation,
There was just untainted innocence, admiration,
kindness and excitement,
You cared, you loved, you tried to do it all your way,
You helped, you survived, you lived to see us do it all our way,
You never asked for anything except warmth, love and company,
Alone, you would fade away but amidst love, your spark would shine brighter than the sun on any given day,
You had a will and were not afraid to say,
You held your own and created your space with love, not hate,
You taught us how to be a family,
You taught us how to live with gratitude, with love, with strength, with a quiet dignity,
Come what may,

These words run freely for those who find a way, to do it all and more, every single day,
Come what may,
These words pour out for those who find a way to dig deeper, every single day,
Come what may,
These words continue to reverberate,
To help, to love, to serve, to pay it forward, always,
Be a beacon of light,
Be a beacon of hope,
Be a beacon of love,
Be a beacon of change,
Come what may.

Sarita Agarwal
09.05.2021

"A selfless and fearless being, a doer, a mother, a father, a brother, a son, a sister, a friend, a daughter, a wife, an aunt, an uncle, a grandmother, a husband, a grandfather, a man, a woman, a girl, a boy, a teacher, a caregiver, a daughter-in-law, a son-in-law, a wife, a healer, a mentor, a guide...A multitude of roles lived out in a lifetime. You carry them all while fighting your inner demons, despite your inner struggles, in spite of it all.

There is a nurturer inside each and every one of us, irrespective of our gender, background or orientation; dig deep, find her and embrace her in all her glory."

THE TREE OF LIFE

The tree speaks to you and me,
Far more often than we can see,
Stop and listen,
Breathe and feel,
Each and every root,
Each and every branch,
Each and every leaf,
Is a reflection of humanity,
The roots go deep into the Earth and keep the tree grounded and upright,
They help store water which is essential for all life,
The branches stretch high and help the leaves create food from sunlight,
Each part serves a purpose,
Each part completes the whole,
Even if one piece falls apart,
That's when the contagion starts,
Each tree is unique,
Each tree is wonderful,
Each tree is powerful,

To recover, the tree must rediscover,
The ability to reconnect with all its elements,
Only when all is in balance,
Only when all is in harmony,
Can the tree lead a life of Synchronicity.

Sarita Agarwal
20.04.2021

MY FAVOURITE PAIR OF JEANS

Currently you remain my favourite pair of jeans,
How or when we part, remains to be seen,
You know me well, as well as anyone can know me,
On my heavy days,
You hug me so like you will never let me go,
On my light days,
You drape me as the water flows,
You make me feel so good,
Without you I would never venture out into the neighbourhood,
You never budge,
You never judge,
On you I can always rely,
If I ever had to let you go, I would surely break down and cry,
I approach the weighing scale with baby steps and look up towards the sky,
I jump for joy as I realise today is not the day I say goodbye,

And so continues my inner tussle seen only by you,
Phew!
Currently you remain my favourite pair of jeans,
How or when we part, remains to be seen.

Sarita Agarwal
18.04.2021

LITTLE BIRDIE

Fly fly fly away,
Little birdie,
You will find your way, come what may,
Fly through the lows and the highs,
Fly up and up into the sky,
Feel the blue upon your wings,
Feel the glow touch your skin,
Feel the light reach your heart,
Feel it all and then restart,
Live live live each day,
Little birdie,
You will find your way, come what may,
Live as if it's your last day,
Live like life's a pinnacle,
Live like life's a miracle,
Little birdie,
You will find yourself in all your glory,
Little birdie,
This is your story.

Sarita Agarwal
16.04.2021

THE KEY

When you feel overwhelmed,
The road is long,
The road is winding,
It never seems to end,
You can't even see the bend,
You need a way,
To ease the pressure that builds up each day,
You look all around you,
But everything confounds you,
There seems to be no end in sight,
Don't give up, Fight!
You will overcome, you will Rise!
If you seek you will find,
All the answers are locked in your heart, soul and mind,
If you seek you will see,
Gratitude and Love are the keys,
To end all miseries.

Sarita Agarwal
13.04.2021

ROAR

A Tilt, A Twirl, A Sway of the hips,
A Bend, A Lift, A Flight of the lips,
A Smile, A Twinkle, A Sprinkle,
Of Love, of Life, of Laughter, of Light,
Of Joy, of Hope, of Peace, of Sheer Delight,
Dance, Fly, Live,Soar
Let the Cosmos hear your Roar!

Sarita Agarwal
06.04.2021

FOR ALL OF ETERNITY

I used to sit waiting for a sign,
Something to show me the road,
The ways of my soul,
The ways of my mind,
Then I met you,
And my heart skipped a beat and two,
Yet I was sceptical,
Could this really be true?
I took my time and you waited patiently,
Till everything became oh so clear to me,
We painted a picture in our past,
So beautiful and wonderful that it will forever last,
As we continue creating moments and memories,
Together we will face what lies ahead joyfully,
You and I are inextricably intertwined,
I am yours and you are mine,
For all of eternity.

Sarita Agarwal
15.03.2021

MY INNER CHILD AND I

With the rising Sun,
Around me, time moves slowly,
Yet to catch up, I am running,
To get things done, I am rushing,
With the setting Sun,
I cannot wait to drop onto my bed,
For night is my favourite time of the day,
As I lay my head on the pillow,
I feel so relaxed and mellow,
As soon as I close my eyes, the child within me comes alive,
To the land of fantasy, magic and mystery, we travel,
We wander, We conquer, We create, We unravel,
And then to my utter dismay,
An infernal ring cuts through,
I am rudely awakened, by the sound of the alarm, from our impending duel,
Oh how could a clock be so cruel?
Another day has dawned,
As I rush to get things done,
I wonder impatiently,
What our fate tonight will be,

With bated breath, on my bed I lay,
My eyes close and I eagerly await,
The mysteries that will come our way,
As I fall into deep slumber,
The child and I travel to the magical realm down under,
We unleash our wands...
And so continues our nocturnal adventure,
Until, alas, once again, the infernal noise doth my dreams enter!
Oh how I wish I could, from waking up, refrain,
In a state of deep slumber forever remain,
Then my inner child and I could stay awake endlessly,
And go on infinite escapades, leisurely.

Sarita Agarwal
14.01.2021

BREATHE IN

It feels like a breath of fresh air,
Somehow, somewhere,
It will dispel the despair,
Along with hope and joy,
It will bring forth a vision of,
A kind of love that we all may care,
A kind of vibe that we all may share,
A kind of life that we all may live,
A kind of warmth that we all may give,
Close your eyes and open up your heart,
Take in a deep breath and start afresh,
Life is what you make it,
Create, Cultivate, Celebrate,
Do it all in the flesh.

Sarita Agarwal
12.01.2021

THE STORM

I feel stuck,
I feel rooted to a spot,
I feel like I'm glued,
I can't seem to be able to move,
At last, I take a few steps with a sense of being free,
And yet, once again, I find myself moved back,
Back to the very spot, where it all began,
I can see it clearly,
As clear as the rain,
Falling relentlessly on the windowpane,
I can see the raindrops rolling down,
Helplessly past the parched ground, unable to quench its thirst,
I am sitting still and yet within me, there is a storm,
My thoughts and my emotions are colliding,
To the set rules they do not want to conform,
Conflict and Contradictions are a bane of my existence,
This war within has become my norm,
Am I really stuck, I wonder?
Am I really rooted to a spot, I wonder?
Am I really glued, I wonder?
As I sit and reflect, a realisation begins to dawn on me,

My choices are my Journey,
My choices are what define Me,
My choices have made Me,
My choices, I embrace Wholly,
I am free to move if I so choose,
I am not bound,
I am surrounded by the ties that bind,
I suddenly feel Unstuck,
Conflict and Contradictions begin to recede into the recesses of my mind,
I can see it all clearly,
As clear as the rain,
Falling gently on the windowpane,
I can see the raindrops rolling down,
I can see them lovingly kiss the parched ground and quench its thirst,
Outside and Within,
The storm has passed.

Sarita Agarwal
23.12.2020

NOW

Where are we now,
Where are we going,
Where are we coming from,
Where will we end up,
So many thoughts race through our heads,
And yet,
Too much is left undone,
Too much is left unsaid,
Let go of your fears,
Take a leap of faith,
Stop thinking of *how* and start *living* instead,
Enjoy being where you are,
Enjoy being who you are,
Enjoy every moment of now,
Enjoy your today,
For in the blink of an eye,
All might become a distant memory,
We can't go back in time and change history,
Now is all we have,
Now is where we must be,

Now is when we must act to the best of our abilities,
To now we must commit wholly,
We may stumble, we might fall,
Or we may soar and conquer it all.

Sarita Agarwal
10.11.2020

WINTER AND I

The flowers blooming on a cold winter morn,
Their fragrance drifting across my face as I walk on,
The tiny specks of sunlight bursting through the clouds,
The cold gentle breeze caressing my cheeks,
The glistening dew drops on the grass and the leaves,
The fluffed-up chests of the squirrels and the birds,
Huddled together giving each other warmth,
My heart is filled with love at these wondrous sights,
And I smile with childlike delight,
Spring fills my world with so much colour,
Summer runs through my veins,
Monsoons, oh how can one not love the rain,
Autumn is the start of all festivities,
And fills the ground with burnt orange leaves,
But there is no season like Winter,
The unparalleled joy of a fresh snowfall,
Is an emotion that needs to be felt by all,
The delicate beauty of snowflakes, each one unique, each
one special, kissing our hair, eyelashes and our face,
The relaxing sound of fire crackling in a fireplace,

The ethereal landscape of the winter sky filled with all shades of a palette,
In this season, nothing is amiss,
Everything is in its place, all perfectly fits,
Winter has stolen my heart, yet I am forever in a state of eternal bliss.

Sarita Agarwal
09.12.2020

I SEE YOU

I still remember being struck by your bright eyes and
your sunny smile,
With each passing year,
I have watched you grow from strength to strength,
I see you now, stronger than ever,
I see you now, taller than ever,
I see you go the extra mile,
I see all the love in your heart,
I see the warmth in your words,
I see the kindness in your embrace,
I see YOU in all that you do,
And I couldn't possibly be more Proud of YOU,
I give thanks and say a prayer everyday for having been
blessed with a sister as beautiful as YOU, inside and out.

Sarita Agarwal
08.12.2020

MY WISH FOR YOU

When I saw you, I was
mesmerized,
I couldn't see past your hair or
your eyes,
When I held you in my arms,
The pain faded, replaced by a
sense of calm,

When I heard you, I rejoiced
at the sweetness of your voice,
You made my heart melt,
I couldn't describe, even if I tried, in that very moment
how I felt,
As time flies by and I see you grow,
My heart is filled with pride and so much more,
My love knows no bounds,
I see a lifetime and beyond,
You make me smile,
You make me proud,
And you also make me shout!

My wishes for you, my children, are immense-
May you be blessed from above,
May you always look upward and onward,
May you choose wisely,
May you of any chains in your path break free,
May you spread your wings and soar,
May you always succeed in everything that you do and help those less fortunate than you,
May your sacred bond grow from strength to strength,
May you always, each other, love, trust, support, honour and defend,
May you always be kind,
May your head and heart always be aligned,
May you always reflect before you speak,
May you always your promises keep,
May you always, in magic, believe,
May you break all boundaries,
May you never waver from your goals or budge,
May you always stay grounded and never judge,
May you live with your entire being,
May your sight be all perceiving,
May you share and be kind to all,
May you love and always be loved by one and all,
May you always rise after every fall.

Sarita Agarwal
01.12.2020

MY REMINISCENCES

Watching the children run to and fro,
Makes my heart glow so,
Brings to my face a smile that is hard to shake,
My thoughts come forth and I float away,
To the days gone by,
I am reminded of the walked miles,
How we took it all in our stride,
The highs and the lows,
The fast and the slow,
The less and the more,
The known and the unknown,
The could and the couldn't,
The did and the didn't,
The ifs and the buts,
The breaks and the heartaches,
The happiness and the excitement,
The curious adventures,
The lasting bonds,
The learnt lessons,
The cherished memories,
All etched into our very soul,
For a lifetime and beyond,

I wouldn't change a thing,
Unparalleled joy to me my reminiscences bring,
As I float back to today,
I wish, I hope, I pray,
They can experience and create it all,
In their own way.

Sarita Agarwal
24.11.2020

IN BLOOM

Go on my love,
All is in bloom,
I have to go, we will meet again soon,
Don't be sad,
Don't be mad,
Make a fresh start,
Let all your worries depart,
Love with all your mind,
Love with all your heart
Love with all your soul,
Don't be blind,
Don't be unkind,
Find your strength,
It flows through your veins,
It flows through mine,
Be strong my love,
Look at the moon up above,
You'll see me waving out,
I'll always be watching over you, without a doubt,
Go on my love,
All is in bloom,
I have to go, we will meet again soon.

Sarita Agarwal
07.11.2020

AN ODE TO MY FATHER

You carry all our worries on your
shoulders,
You carry all our love in your arms,
You will walk till the end of
the world to ensure we are
not harmed,
You do all that you can, even when things fall through
despite best-laid plans,
You smile through all your pain,
You smile even when all appears to be in vain,
We see the light shining in your eyes,
Your strength speaks to us through your words that are
wise,
Never look back my dear children, they say,
Carry on forward, lies ahead the way.

Sarita Agarwal
22.11.2020

THE SIGHT

I was swimming towards the horizon, as far as my eyes could see,
I wanted to reach the point where all ends appear to meet,
I swam too far out and now I am lost in the middle of the deep,
I can only see the endless blue ocean all around me,
My body is heavy and my spirit feels weighed down,
I try to shout but there is no sound,
I lie back looking up at the sky,
I see the world spinning, life passing me by,
I want to catch up, not be left behind,
I am searching for a boat to help me stay afloat,
I am searching for an anchor to hold me fast in the impending storm,
I am searching for a rope to pull me ashore,
I am searching for a way to not drown,
I am searching for a lifeline in any form,
I am searching for hope to give me strength to hold on,
It would be so easy to sail away as the wind blows,
It would be so easy to flow away as the water flows,
It would be so easy to loosen my grip and let it all go,

So easy,
It would be,
So easy,
It could be,
So easy,
But should it be?
No! I don't want to give in,
No! I don't want to give up,
Pull me into the shallow from the deep end,
Pull me up back to the surface,
I want to survive,
I want to carry on,
I will sink no more,
I am lifting the veil that is blocking my vision,
I can see the horizon,
I can see the shore,
I can see the changes that I need to make,
I can see the path that I need to take,
I can see what is and not what appears to be,
I can see it all so seamlessly,
I can see where I am,
I am exactly where I am meant to be.

Sarita Agarwal
07.11.2020

PAPER PLANE

To float away into the air without a care,
To fly any way or anywhere,
Without anyone steering me, completely on my own, direction free,
With just a little force, I push off,
I feel light, I let my imagination carry me,
To conquer all that I cannot imagine,
To conquer all that I cannot fathom,
To higher heights, to deeper depths,
Through difficult paths, through the ones easy to tread,
Oh, is this how it would feel to be a paper plane,
I can go on till the very end,
Fly away, float away, without a need to comprehend,
The way of life, the ways of our existence,
Oh, let me be a paper plane and fly away without any resistance.

Sarita Agarwal
13.11.2020

WIDE AWAKE

We are created out of love,
We are nourished in the womb,
We are reborn at birth,
Our first breath outside,
Our first sound, a loud cry, announces that we are alive,
Soon there are firsts of many,
Our first hug,
Our first laugh,
Our first word,
Our first crawl,
Our first tooth,
Our first step,
Our first stumble,
Our first dash across the room,
Our first taste of pain as we tumble,
Our first jump for joy when we learn there is so much more to explore,
We find our rhythm and things begin to fall into place,
We are happy, carefree, content in our own space,
And then the polarity of life slowly seeps in,
Lack of contentment begins to dig its claws deep within,
Our *needs* begin to wander toward *wants* constantly,

Our gaze wavers from the joy of discovery to a greed to forever compete,
We no longer share or care,
We are consumed by an urge to judge and compare,
We succeed but there is no satisfaction in the success,
Deep down we all know something is amiss,
There is no passion, there is no emotion,there is no connection,
With our skin or with our actions,
Akin to dormant beings, we function,
Our body moves,our mind is active but our soul has slipped into a state of deep sleep,
Tired of constantly being bombarded with what we desire and think we need,
Look anew, this is where we have always been,
Look around and hear all the sounds,
Look around and see all that surrounds,
Look around and drink it all in,
Each tells a story that hasn't been penned down,
Each and every page needs to be read out loud,
To shake things up,
To stir things up,
To wake things up,
To awaken us,
To awaken you and me,
I can hear, I can see, I can read,
All is loud, All is clear,
I am wide awake, are you, my dear?

Sarita Agarwal
31.10.2020

ONE AND ONLY

I feel free even when situations
imprison me,
I see hope even when I am
down a slippery slope,
I see magic even when life plays
a trick,
I feel relief even when I'm
standing on the edge of a cliff,
I see the answer in every
blooming flower,
I see the light even on a moonless night,
I see reason even through treason,
I see the gain despite deep pain,
I feel alive even when our worlds collide,
I see the start even when things fall apart,
My rise after every fall comes as no surprise,
My Always and Forever,
My Friend, My lover,
My Four Leaf Clover,
My One and Only,
Because YOU are with me.

Sarita Agarwal
30.10.2020

IN THIS MOMENT

Waking up alone,
I feel so torn,
I remember your touch,
I take in your smell,
I feel you beside me still,
Asking me to move on,
Now, walking all alone,
I feel the weight of every step,
The distance seems too long,
The trees are in Autumn,
The air feels heavy and the sky looks grey,
I find our favourite bench,
I sit down to catch my breath,
I close my eyes and I see You,
The smile in your eyes,
The gentle touch of your lips,
Your arms around me,
The love in your laughter as you lift your chin,
To tuck me in tighter,
I want us to be together,
I want this moment to last forever,
As my eyelids start to quiver,

I feel a hand on my shoulder,
I turn around to see you,
Standing behind me,
I rush to embrace you,
I rush to feel your face,
I rush to feel your skin,
I rush to feel your hair,
You see the urgency in every touch,
And hold me tight and tuck me into your world,
You whisper in my ear,
There is nothing to fear,
I'll always be around, now I am here,
We hold each other's hands and start to walk,
Every step is light but the distance seems too short,
The trees are in bloom and the air flows over with floral fragrance,
The sky is all shades of the rainbow,
As if a child has let his soul run free,
With paints of all colours on his canvas,
My spirit is lifted and I feel at ease,
Our heart flows over with hope,
Our heart flows over with joy,
Our heart flows over with love,
In this moment, for all of eternity.

Sarita Agarwal
30.10.2020

THEN AND NOW

Heavy is my body
Heavy is my mind,
Heavy is my soul,
Heavy I feel,
Heavy I think,
Dragging my feet I slump onto the bed,
Sinking down low, as low as low can go,
Heavy as I lay,
Right down to my very core,
Curled up tight, as tight as tight can get,
Stop! I tell these thoughts flowing through my head,
Alas! they don't pay heed and spill over into my heart,
Like the cotton seed that is whisked from its branch,
Carried away by the wind once it's dried and ready to part,
Change is inevitable,
Change is the only constant,
What goes Up must come Down,
There is a Grin for every Frown,
There is no Then without Now,
There is no Joy without Sorrow,
Every day is Yesterday, Today and Tomorrow,

Like everything else, this heaviness too shall pass,
In time, I float back to the surface,
Light is my body,
Light is my mind,
Light is my soul,
Light I feel,
Light I think,
As I rise out of bed and jump to my feet,
Light as I stand,
Right down to my very core,
Now there is a lightness to my being until I feel
more……

Sarita Agarwal
24.10.2020

SAY A PRAYER FOR US

I pray for each and
every one of us who
has a Voice,
I pray for the
Voiceless,
I pray for each and
every one of us who
has Power,
I pray for the
Powerless,
I pray for each and every one of us who is blessed with
Abundance,
I pray for those suffering from Scarcity,
I pray for each and every one of us who is a Perpetrator,
I pray for the Victims,
I pray for each and every one of us who is a Believer,
I pray for the Apostates,
I pray for Limitless Starlight,
I pray for Endless Sunshine,
I pray for Boundless Moonbeams,
I pray for Untouched Oceans,
I pray for Pristine Rivers,

I pray for Unblemished Glaciers,
I pray for Green Forests,
I pray for the Deepest Depths of Earth to remain Unseen,
I pray for Humanity,
I pray for all Species,
I pray for All Beings,
I pray we see Ourselves in the Other,
I pray we Recognise the Duality of our World,
I pray we Re-Unite,
I pray we Recover from this Self-Created Plight.

Sarita Agarwal
19.10.2020

THE PASSING

Falling, Crashing, Sinking,
How am I still standing?
Trying to find the right words to ease the pain, though in vain,
Trying to somehow make sense of this loss,
Trying to find someone, something to blame at all costs,
Knowing deep inside I have to bear my own cross,
Surrounded by people, yet I feel alone,
My heart is in pieces, my mind is on a journey of its own,
My thoughts begin to drift as they see fit,
I wonder what it will feel like,
I wonder what it will be like,
I wonder, will I speak or not say,
I wonder, will it be night or day,
I wonder, will it be spring or summer,
I wonder, will it be in the midst of winter,
I wonder, will I know before it happens,
I wonder, will it be quick or the pace will slacken,
I wonder, will I be able to say goodbye,
I wonder, will I let go or hold on tight,
I wonder, will I be scared or anxious,

I wonder, will I be at peace or fractious,
I wonder, will it be the end or just a cross over,
I wonder, will things be left open-ended or will I find closure,
As I wonder what lies ahead,
Another thought races through my head,
The past has passed its history,
The future cannot be known with certainty,
The present is where we are alive,
Hug each other, love each other, always be kind,
Be loud, Be heard, live with all your might,
Step out of your thoughts, step out of your mind,
Don't waste another moment of this precious gift called 'Life'.

Sarita Agarwal
13.10.2020

OUTER COVER

We are one, We are the same,
Appearances are unimportant, relevant only in name,
This is what I was taught,
This is the absolute truth I thought,
Life was like a fairytale, nothing could go wrong,
And then he came along,
At first I was so excited to see,
Another being, another extension of me,
We played, We fought, We laughed, We cried,
Together, we hoped,
Together, we wished,
Together, we dreamed,
Of climbing each mountain,
Of touching the sky,
Of covering the vast expanse of this land,
Soon we came to a realisation first-hand,
We noticed the looks,
We heard the whispers,
We began to feel the segregation,
We began to realise the separation,
They are not alike, she is different,
He is fair, she is a darker shade of grey,

Light or dark, for a boy it doesn't matter,
The 'prospects' greatly reduce for a girl, if not completely shatter,
For a boy the world is served on a platter,
For a girl, from birth itself life is so much harder,
Us and Them? Dark and Fair? Boy and Girl? Man and Woman? She and Him?
Unbridled anger made our head spin,
The world as we knew it, seemed to be falling apart,
How I wish we could glue it back together and make a fresh start,
From this awareness there is no going back,
Slowly we pieced it all together and saw a spark,
The light at the end of a tunnel that seemed dark,
Can they be blamed for their thoughts?
The separateness that everyone spews is not new,
It has been passed down from generations to me and you,
All Questions and Rebellions suppressed,
Without any hesitation with an iron fist,
We question you now,We have regained our focus,
Who are you to brand us?
Will our gender and skin stop us from doing what we love?
Will our gender and skin stop us from achieving our dreams?
Will our gender and skin stop us from being who we want to be?
Will our gender and skin stop us from becoming humane beings?

They who give importance to gender,
They who give credence to colour,
They who judge us by our outer cover,
You are the ones with a dark mind and heart,
We have allowed you to obstruct our path,
You are the ones we will outlast,
I am *I* and He is *he*,
Together we create unity,
Each with our own unique abilities,
Each different with the same Identity,
Our gender and Our skin are an extension of US,
Our thoughts, Our actions, Our words,
Show who we are, reflect our true worth,
No more!
Here and now ends all division,
We will no longer live in isolation,
We will no longer allow any form of discrimination,
We can clearly identify the false prophets,
We can see through their empty promises,
We will rise above all Prejudices,
We will not bow down, we will not give in,
We are one, we are Kin,
We are together, We are each other,
We will no longer be oppressed because of our Outer Cover!

Sarita Agarwal
09.10.2020

LOVE

When I look at you all I see is Love,
When I look at you all I feel is Love,
When I look at you all I hear is Love,
When I look at you all I know is Love,
When I look at you all I think is Love,
When I look at you all I need is Love,
When I look at you all I breathe is Love,
When you see me,
When you feel me,
When you hear me,
When you know me,
When you think of me,
When you need me,
When you breathe me in and lift me up into your arms,
All we create is LOVE.

Sarita Agarwal
06.10.2020

THE PHYSICAL PLANE

The first thing that we see when we open our eyes,
With each movement, with each step,
We grow, we love, we experience it all,
Each day together, side by side,
The bond is strong, it feels like it will be lifelong,
As our universe expands and we seek out more,
We slowly begin to go our separate ways,
Caught up in creating another world,
We fall out of touch,
Our frequency is lost,
The meets are less, the talks are lesser,
Slowly the bond appears to be weaker,
Not intentionally, but sometimes we grow apart,
In the flesh but not in one's heart,
As it must, life continues,
One day you wake up to hear the news,
Without warning, straight out of the blue,
The world crumbles around you,
The pain is unimaginable, it cuts through you like a knife,
Deep into the very depths of your soul,
Never again can you feel whole,

This loss is permanent, this separation is final,
You can't retrace your steps,
You can never go back,
To how it was or how it could ever be,
With the passage of time, the pain begins to heal,
You remember the cherished moments,
You relive the beautiful memories,
You and I may never meet again on the Physical Plane,
Connected in Mind, Soul and Spirit,
We shall forever remain.

Sarita Agarwal
05.10.2020

SISTERHOOD

When I close my eyes and think of the years gone by,
I remember how you stood beside me in,
The hard times,
The uncertainties,
I remember how we shared a smile in,
The good times,
The certainties,
I remember how you
Showed me love and kindness,
No matter what, I always had your support,
As we grow older,
Our love continues to grow deeper,
Our bond turns stronger,
Seasons come and go,
Time will pass us by,
But Sisterhood is timeless, sisters are for life.

Sarita Agarwal
27.09.2020

THE FORGOTTEN

Gazing over the hills,
As far as the naked eye can see,
Sitting,absorbing, thinking,
Taking in the stillness of it all,
In my mind's eye, I see life rushing by,
Always on the move, running uphill,
The pace is fast, we don't sit still,
Unable to savour what Is,
As we constantly seek what's next,
In the pursuit of Tomorrow, Today is left behind,
In the midst of nature, the pace is tranquil,
The wispy clouds are adrift,
The soft wind whispers soundlessly,
The willowy trees sway in the breeze,
The butterflies and the dragon flies dance a delightful dance,
The Cicadas chirp with carefree abandon,
The buzzing bees gleefully seek out nectar from blooms,
The birds sing their songs, each with its own lyric and melody,
In it all,
There is rhythm, there is movement, there is motion,

Each deliberate, unhurried, steady, leisurely,
There is reason, there is purpose, there is conclusion,
All untouched, unblemished, undamaged,
unbound,unconfined,
In this moment, I am a part of this liberation,
But I wonder if I am truly free?
A fear lurks deep within,
Can it forever so remain?
There is no escape from the truth of our existence,
Of all that we could be, we are merely a semblance,
We have become the Forgotten,
Unremembered how to live,
Abandoned the value of being born human,
Remember who you are,
Remind yourself of all that you can be,
Only then can we,
Truly Hear,
Truly Feel,
Truly See,
As I look up towards the endless sky,
A cool,gentle breeze caresses my cheek,
The Sun's light radiates far and wide,
Inch by inch, it reaches me,
The fear is disappearing,
The Forgotten are remembering,
I begin to smile,
I am finally free,
Within and outside.

Sarita Agarwal
29.09.2020

MY WORLD

There she is,
Sitting opposite me,
Eyes wide open with wonder,
Looking at me sincerely,
Taking in each spoken word earnestly,
Asking intricate questions about life,
Waiting impatiently for all the answers she thinks I have,
To soothe her childlike curiosity I respond to a few,
The ones I cannot answer, I try to eschew,
Not too long ago she was in my lap,
Cooing, gurgling, laughing,
Lying on her back,
Soon she was crawling, walking, running,
Climbing on my back,
She was my world and I was her all,
As she grows older and begins to explore,
I can see her universe expanding beyond me to so much more,
Oh how I wish it wasn't so but I know I need to learn to let her go,
Out into the cosmos to become all that she can be,
I have held her hand for as long as I can,

Watched over her closely from afar,
To see she gets back up after every fall,
Helped her find the path she needs to walk alone,
As I watch her now, still closely from afar,
Enjoying life and its uncertainties with ease,
My heart swells with pride, I can't contain my smile,
She is my world and so it will always be,
This is one of life's certainties.
"The everlasting bond between parent and child"

Sarita Agarwal
20.09.2020

FIT OF TERROR

I am cracking..
I am crying..
I am choking..
I am dying..
I can't breathe..
I can't feel..
I can't see..
I can't speak..
The ceiling is collapsing..
The walls are closing in..
The floor begins to shake..
The Dark is darkening..
I crouch in a corner..
My heart beats outside my chest..
My head on my knees..
My feet begin to slip..
My hands hold on tight..
Crushing me with all their might..
Rocking hurriedly from side to side..
Counting hastily..

One, two, three, four, five..six, seven, eight, nine, ten…
My mind stops racing,
The light cuts through the darkness within,
Everything is as it should be,
I can finally see again,
Today I have succeeded in keeping anxiety at bay,
But Tomorrow is another day,
I will conquer Fit of Terror,
I am ready, my fight will resume,
The Battle has been won but the War continues…..

"Panic attacks are unprovoked and unpredictable. People experiencing an attack are seized with terror and fear. On the surface, symptoms vary from chest pain to shortness of breath, uncontrollable trembling, profuse sweating, an inability to speak. Within, they range from an impending sense of doom to fear of death, pounding heart rate, claustrophobia and more. On top of all this, people start worrying about when the next attack will occur. This is known as 'anticipatory anxiety'. Panic attacks, Panic disorder and Fit of Terror are just a few terms that are used to describe these emotions. Panic attacks are real and the struggle is daily. The cases have skyrocketed during the pandemic and more children and adolescents are experiencing them as well as adults. This is extremely alarming.

Recognise the symptoms,be aware of your triggers, find a coping mechanism that works for you—read, write, listen to music, dance, laugh, practice pranayam, talk, reach out and create a support system. Have a network of close confidants who you can call anytime, take the help and pay it forward. Eat healthy, nutritious food and remember to sleep well.

Love yourself, take care of you."

Sarita Agarwal
20.09.2020

ALCHEMY OF LOVE

How do I find thee,
When do I begin to see,
All that we can be,
Stumbling, trying to put the pieces together,
Removing layer after layer, to get a clearer picture,
Of a tender, alive, humane being that lies beneath the surface,
Not someone who lacks a sense of self or purpose,
All this time spent closely to ensure,
What we share is true and pure,
Will we ever surely know if love can forever last?
Is it meant to surpass all that lies in its path?
Does the heart stop beating after every beat?
Do the lungs stop breathing after every breath?
Does the mind stop thinking after every thought?
Reach within, bare your soul, explore,
Be honest, be brave, reveal your innermost traits,
When you see in your eyes,with love,
Your Self reflected truly,
Then you know you have answered life's greatest query,
You are love and love is thee,
Together, you will surpass all that lies in your path,
Together, you will forever last.

Sarita Agarwal
19.09.2020

MUSIC AND I

When I am feeling low,
Music makes me soar,
Beyond the clouds and more,
Leaving all behind,
That which makes me pine,
When I hear a tune play,
My feet begin to move and my body starts to sway,
As I hear the lyrics, my voice escapes my lips,
The songs embrace my heart and soul,
Each melody makes me whole,
With Music, I declare, my constant love affair,
You captivate the deepest recesses of my mind,
We are forever inseparably intertwined.

Sarita Agarwal
18.09.2020

"The possibilities of Music are endless. It transports us to another realm, helps us feel, heal, create and escape, if we so desire. Music, I love thee endlessly"

WHEN YOU LOOKED AT ME

When you looked at me,
I saw the love in your eyes,
I felt the warmth in your embrace,
I heard the excitement in your whisper,
When you look at me now,
I see the loathing in your eyes,
I feel the iciness in your embrace,
I hear the indifference in your whisper,
In the same room and yet worlds apart,
So much to say and yet we cannot start,
This incommunicable pain,
This reluctance to share or explain,
How have we come to be,
These unrecognisable, separate entities?

Sarita Agarwal
14.09.2020

THE ETERNAL YEARNING

The Rising Sun shines so bright
Its light does not differentiate,
The rays reach far and wide,
Permeate all, hidden and in sight,
The setting Sun steps away to reveal the Moon,
Waiting patiently,
At times waxing, at times waning,
The light pervades the darkness,
Pushing away the gloom,
And this cycle continues,
Connected eternally yet never to meet,
Oh, how painful is this yearning and yet,so sweet ……

Sarita Agarwal
21.08.2020

THE WAR WITHIN

Raw words, inner conflictions
Start conversations, end conversations,
An outpouring of the purest of emotions,
Deepest thoughts, darkest desires and fears,
They control us, they move us to tears,
Let it all out, let it go, don't hold back,
Feel the release, feel the lightness,
As you slowly but surely recognise the cracks,
Reach out and pull yourself together,
Don't hesitate to confide in another,
This is the beginning, not the end
Life is a beautiful journey of self-discovery, my friend.

Sarita Agarwal
22.08.2020

YOUNG LOVE

Short sharp breaths,
Tightening of the chest,
Heaving bosom,
Quickening of the heart,
Curling toes,
Butterflies in the belly,
Sweaty palms,
Impatient fingers,
Quivering eyelids,
Flushing cheeks,
Sweetness of lips,
The slight upturned corner of the mouth,
Stolen glances, stolen kisses, stolen moments,
Oh,to be young and fall in love all over again ......

Sarita Agarwal
04.09.2020

WANDERLUST

Golden rays,
The deep blue sky,
Filled with wispy clouds,
Full of infinite hues,
Silvery moonlight,
The sparkling stars,
The chorus of soaring birds,
The whispering of willowy trees,
The ebbing of the ocean tide,
The gently flowing river,
Call out to me,
"Join us, be free,
Life is full of limitless possibilities,
Delight in the timelessness of its journey,
Seemingly without purpose,
Yet wholly with intention"
I am consumed by this wanderlust.......

Sarita Agarwal
06.09.2020

BELIEVE

Gaea is our God,
Nature our Religion,
And Terra our house of worship,
Known by many names,
A Temple, A Church, A Shrine,
A Mosque, A Synagogue, A Tabernacle,
A Gurdwara, A Cathedral….,
Animals, Birds, Insects are the Believers,
Humans are the Non-Believers,
Where do we stand,who are we?
Look around you and see,
There is violence, war, death, damage and destruction,
We pollute, cause pain, hate and divisions,
We refuse to learn from our past lessons,
We let our Ego and Greed make all the decisions,
Where does this lead us?
Where does this leave us?
If we truly begin to Believe,
The sky will turn blue,
Clean air we will breathe,
The water, the soil will again be pristine,
Slowly but surely Earth will Heal.

Sarita Agarwal
08.09.2020

AN ODE TO COVID

Let's face it,
Covid is here to stay,
The reasons range from one to many,
It's made us count our Blessings and our Pennies,
Let's face it,
We can't carry on as we may,
We must look within and change our ways,
Let's face it,
May we use this as a time to Heal,
May we relearn how to love, care, think and feel.

Sarita Agarwal
12.08.2020

STOP RUNNING

I Stepped away
From the pleasant embrace that terrified me,
From the comfortable piece of cloth that suffocated me,
From the secure doors that caged me,
I Moved
Towards the uncharted, the unfamiliar and the unseen,
I Moved
Away from the Illusory Light that casts its sheen
On the known, the familiar and the seen,
Towards the misconstrued darkness that obscures all that lies in-between,
Somehow
I broke out of the embrace,
Somehow
I tore away the piece of cloth,
Somehow
I opened the doors,
Somehow
I broke free from all that had been,
Without looking back,
With no baggage in tow,
I walked, I ran, I sprinted,

Resolute and relentless, I persisted,
As my pace began to slow
Called out The Vast Unknown-
"Come and sit with me a while,
Catch your breath, close your eyes,
Rest your weary heart and soul,
Pause, ponder, watch your life unfold,
Let there be of self-love and self-care no dearth,
YOU must truly believe in your worth,
Listen to your inner voice,
Take the risks, make the hard choice,
Own your decisions,
Break the illusion,
Clear your vision,
Safe is a state of mind,
It's not a person,
It's not a place,
It's not any form of give and take,
Safe is how we feel inside,
Beloved child, forever in my loving embrace,
Stop Running, YOU are SAFE."

Sarita Agarwal
27.11.2024

GAS CHAMBER

Tired bodies, weary minds,
Looking around, trying to find,
A way to soothe their aching souls,
Instead they fall deeper into a deep,dark hole,
Endlessly spiralling out of control,
Trying to catch their breath but to no avail,
Breathless, gasping, destined to fail,
The heartbeats grow louder and louder,
The screams scream "Bloody murder",
Stuck inside this Gas Chamber,
Without an out in sight,
A realisation dawning,
They are alone in their plight,
Tired bodies, weary minds,
Looking around, trying to find,
If this ache could ever abate,
Slowly but surely resigning themselves to their
impending fate ....

Sarita Agarwal
27.11.2024

Printed by Libri Plureos GmbH in Hamburg, Germany

9 789369 540655